you can't keep it

poems

k.b. marie

This book is a product of the author's imagination. Any references to historical events, real people, or real places have been used fictitiously. Other names, characters, places, and incidents are also the product of the author's imagination. Any resemblance to actual persons, living or dead, business establishments, events, or locales is entirely coincidental.

No part of this book shall be reproduced or transmitted in any form or by any means without prior written permission of the publisher. Although every precaution has been taken in preparation of the book, the publisher and the author assume no responsibility for errors or omissions. Neither is any liability assumed for damages resulting from the use of information contained in this book or its misuse.

Copyright © 2020 K.B. Marie
Illustrations by Victoria Solomon
Formatting by Jasie Gale
All rights reserved.

ISBN-13: 978-1-949577-37-2
ISBN-10: 1-949577-37-6

you can't keep it

table of contents

lighten up	9

I.
so your mother disappoints you	13
kwan yin, mother of mercy	16
tell me	18
the price	20
inside the lines	22
the theory of us	23
anxiety	25
last day of the month	26
duality in the daytime	27
duality in the nighttime	28
uncertainty	30
it's easier looking out	33
long afternoons in lockdown	34
politics	35
ouija board	36
amends	38
to the uncle that hit us	41
the rabbit also comes at dusk	42

II.
wheel of fortune	47
mary oliver	48
does it matter	50
father	52

forgiveness	53
go on	55
3:16 a.m.	57
what's going to happen	59
we do what we can	61
roulette	62
divination	63
settle in for the long haul	64
hyacinth	65
first light	66
yet here I am, here I am reaching	67
knowing is a mask (fear wears)	70
no carry-on baggage	72

III.

you called to ask for money again	77
when pride lifts her mask	79
imperfect	80
the wisdom of no escape	82
this	85
god	86
mala	89
you can't keep it	90
reincarnation	93
the merits	95
snow in april	98
surrender	99
ode to winter	102

For Leitha,
my mother

lighten up

The crows are harassing the hawk again.
They swoop, they dive, they fall over themselves
laughing. It doesn't matter that talons are sharp.

It doesn't matter how deadly
this flirtation can be. Even now
they're losing their minds with happiness.

They beg me to do the same.
All the world is a game, they say.
The same is true for you.

Perhaps I was born to survive this.
Perhaps I was born only with the ambition
to remake myself, again and again—

the way the oak remakes itself each spring.
Whether it's an acorn, dark and dormant.
Or tall and proud in its gray suit,
Or cut through and hollowed—

every moment, every breath—it's still in the game.
And after everything, so am I.

I.

so your mother disappoints you

1.

So your mother disappoints you
and it's hard not to take it personally.
She drinks a twelve pack and drives
45 miles in the wrong direction, away
from the elementary school where
you sing a song about a heart
while yours is breaking. Alone,
overlooking the sea of faces
you don't know. Or Thanksgiving
when most children gather around
the dinner table, say *grace* and *thank you*
for the mothers who spoon out greens
and cranberries onto white plates
while you walk into the jailhouse.
Hands up, pat down, and the plexiglass
remains between you. When she calls
to say she can't leave him because
she has nowhere to go. Yes, it's hard
not to take it personally in a world of
a thousand choices—
and not one of them is you.

2.

But then I think of the valley, the forest
rich with life though trapped in the canyon.
Lightning strikes there often. A brush fire
springs up, sweeps through the pines.
Animals are killed, a river polluted, and
the sky darkened with ash. One feels as if
all is lost. Nothing will ever be the same.
One could say *how terrible, how tragic* when
considering the burned paws. Or one
can also see the transformation in it. The burn
is needed. The burn brings growth.
The burn is the only reason the valley thrives.

3.

There's one missing fact: It's not about me.
When the muscle, tired, fails,
one cannot blame the body,
however attached. I came from your flesh
but now separate, I might as well be a
crane, white wings erect, lifting away.
I made the mistake of thinking the glass
was gone between us—that your
decisions were still yoked to mine.

How can I hate you for staying behind,
when I've yet to find the courage to leave you?

kwan yin, mother of mercy

I don't know why I'm sad.
I don't know why I'm crying.

I can only tell you

that there is a river
rock where my heart should be.
It's cold and rubbed smooth

by time. But the river is gone now.
Only the lack remains.

Sadness feels like the last light
of day, a melancholy whispered
through the trees as the last leaf
of autumn tumbles

to the ground. Sadness is a path
in the dark and we all must walk it.
Sadness is a light ahead, a promise
of what is coming, knowing

I can never turn back.

All I ask is that you stay with me,
here in this wild forest of our making.

And please
hold me tight if I try to run.

tell me

I am obsessed with the past
lives. I beg the soul
for dreams, for memories.

Was I a scholar, riding
across a desert in search
of ink-truth scrolls?

Was I a queen contending
with her court's pretenders?
Perhaps a would-be socialite

in New York, living
in the hollow excess of
the loneliness I still carry.

A theater rat.
More rags than meals. A street
runner with a stone bed.

Was I a poor Irish girl
washing my clothes
in the cold stream? Did I

enjoy a single, beautiful day
before the storm…

                    Tell me.

Tell me, please.
I must know what I was,
what I can survive, if I'm to go on.

the price

i...
i...
i...

Writing that feels shameful.
It feels like betrayal.

A scarlet letter from the trailer park
where I was born.

Poverty must be educated out of you.
Want must be educated out of you.
Woman must be educated out of you.

You will accept only *I* white-washed in a top-hat of gold.

It makes no difference what I was before.
This is what you've made of me. Conformity
is standing on the other side of the river
forever washed of our sins.

I have survived but at what price. How much will
this box cost me? Can I make myself small enough
to fit in a pocket so that *I* may guarantee
my safe passage, anywhere, anytime?

I must ask because I learned this truth as a child:

There are simply some places I'm not welcome.

And when I must go to these places I leave myself at home.
I can't help but think of her though.
Often alone in a sea of faces, I wonder about *i i i i i*

I wonder, where is she now?

inside the lines

Why is it easier to walk on the sidewalk than to cut across the grass? Why is it harder to mount the hill

and lie beneath the blue sky, knowing that passing cars can see me, witness my communion? It's more

difficult to give myself permission to be here alone in a park that my taxes paid for than to follow where the street signs direct me.

Check all boxes. Sign here. Retouch the fading lines.

I step out the door only to count how many turns it will take until I am home again.

Walk faster, little dog. We're a nuisance when we wander.

How can I still want so much and fear it more?

the theory of us

We're given bodies and agency
to sleep, wake, and dream.
And legs that lead us to believe
we can go where we please.
But what of the orbit?
The gravity of the collapsed star
in our chests, producing enough
disruption to wing-pin us in place?
Clothed only by our willful fears,
I don't blame us. Not even
the worst of us, for all these faults,
these furies. We're given
the world and then taught how
small, how reduced,
one must be to endure it.

anxiety

The chipmunk plays, refreshed
by the morning frost. He has more
food than he can carry
in his puffed cheeks. The sun
warms his sable fur. He is free.
He can go anywhere he pleases.

So why must I look to the sky, searching,
waiting always for the hawk's shadow
to cut across the ground?

last day of the month

Bills always come due.
I spread the papers on the table.
I run the math again. I look
into the future, gathering
where I can, courage. What goes
out, what comes in—it's all reduced
to the singular hum
of the flexing mind, a grasping
for any branch extended above
this river. But the water moves
too fast here. The counting
becomes a prayer, softly
murmured. A last breath
as the edge and promised drop
arrives, consuming my view.

duality in the daytime

The chipmunks chase each other in the garden.
I sit at the dining table, sad.

Goldfinches swing in the zinnias, while
I sniffle and pout.

The little dog at my feet brings his favorite toy
but I turn my head from wet cheek to cheek.

A robin coos a sweet melody,
a child laughs,
sunlight stretches languidly along the polished floor.

But I can do nothing better than cry,
count the dead, wonder
what in the world will we eat tomorrow?

The world says we have so much here, so much
to smile for. Yet here I am, having none of it.

duality in the nighttime

Sleeping is supposed to be easy now.
All the lights are off.

All the screaming children
and yapping dogs, and unhappy couples

have taken to their beds.
Deer roam the garden, sure.

Racoons sift through the compost bin.
But what can be put away has been

put away. That leaves me. Awake
and wishing the knot in my back

would let go. It can't. It's holding on
for dear life to fears intent on

traveling up my spine and nesting
in my machine of a brain. A machine

built to process, built to work it all out.
I should be thankful for this, that this

foreman of spinal nerves has stemmed
the flow. A gift, this moment alone

with me, this bed, a snoring dog
and a warm wife. A moment of peace—

or it would be. If only I wasn't awake
listening to all these gears turning.

uncertainty

I thought answers meant peace.
I thought following
the string of my own desire

would deliver me to solid ground,
ground where I could
put both feet. I must've
taken a wrong turn

somewhere. This is geometry
of the soul. I work
the angles and arrive

where I started. The danger
of oversimplification
is that you only become

aware of where you are
once you are no longer there.

I know I'm turned around.

Don't tell me
this is about the journey,
not the destination.

I'm trying to get

somewhere, buddy, even
if you aren't. I can't

begin because I've forgotten
something. Something
essential. "What is it?"

I ask the hand on the handle
of an exit that doesn't exist.

"Please tell me. What is it
I'm looking for?"

it's easier looking out

It must be raining. I can't see it myself
but the sun is gone and the people

hurry past my window with umbrellas up
and jackets clasped beneath their chins.

I can see the magnolia though, pink
blossoms swaying in the wind, lifting

as if groped by a rough hand, falling
as if forgotten. Crushed petals

create a path, a trail leading to—
ah, I hear it now.

The soft tapping against the window.
See the droplets spreading out in the dark

bird bath, removing all reflections.
Is the light on the horizon moving

toward me or away? Is an answer
really so much to ask for?

long afternoons in lockdown

An unseen hand strikes
the piano. The keys discordant
cry out. The ringing builds
in my ears, seems to feed itself
with itself. All I want is
a melody. A rhythm.
A predictable beginning,
middle, and end. I want
a chorus I wrap myself up in,
and sing along with. Lyrics
I can memorize so that when
the song comes on the radio
again—and there is always an *again*—
then I will know where I am
and more importantly,
I'll know where this is going.

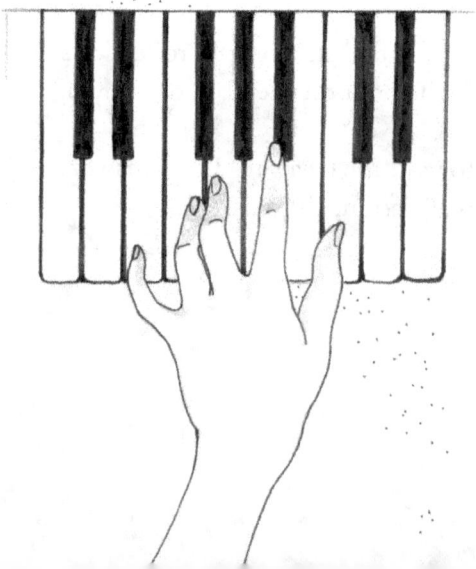

politics

I'm awakened in the night by something
screaming. A prey fights.

It doesn't want to be eaten. As I lie
in the dark, listening, I wonder

what's my part in this? One wants only
to eat. The other

wants only to not be eaten.
And there is so much here I don't

understand. About seasons, systems,
about the interplay of power and

balance. About what my action will do—
for better or worse. What we think

will make things better, often
does not make things better.

Go back to bed. Open the window.
Choose a side. Or let resolution bloom

like jasmine in the night…
It's no wonder I don't sleep anymore.

ouija board

When it came, it was black, true,
but it sparkled, iridescent.
If I were braver, I'd call it
beautiful. Honestly,
it could have been anything:

A shadow passing over
the wide-eyed face of the moon,
a blood vessel in my eye,
constricting, the flicker
of a half-spent bulb.

But it called itself, *demon*.
It called me *light, temple*.

It freely admitted it lives for pain.
Yet, I welcomed it. I listened.
And though I was not afraid,
I can't help but question:

how often do we tell the truth
about ourselves?

If I refuse to believe in something
can I make *anything* less real?

amends

After her death, I spoke to my grandmother
more than I had in years. I relived

brushing her coarse hair
with my baby hands, touching

the knot on the back of her skull. Her
rolling an orange along the table,

softening the meat inside, cutting
a hole in its top for me to drink.

Peeling an apple, adding salt,
dusting an overturned water glass,

cutting biscuits from softly punched dough.
She'd flick the end of her cigarette

and smile. Half demon, half angel
of those endless Tennessee summers stretched

long by memory. All green grass, and church
Sundays, painted eggs, and the lone maple tree.

Tracy Chapman's *Give Me One Reason
to Stay Here,* played through open windows.

But that was thirty years ago. The music
has since been replaced with gasping,

the oranges with burning spoons. That house
is filled with bottles, with hands fisting in hair.

I'm sorry I let all that keep me away, I tell her.
In her voice, *there's nothing left to forgive.*

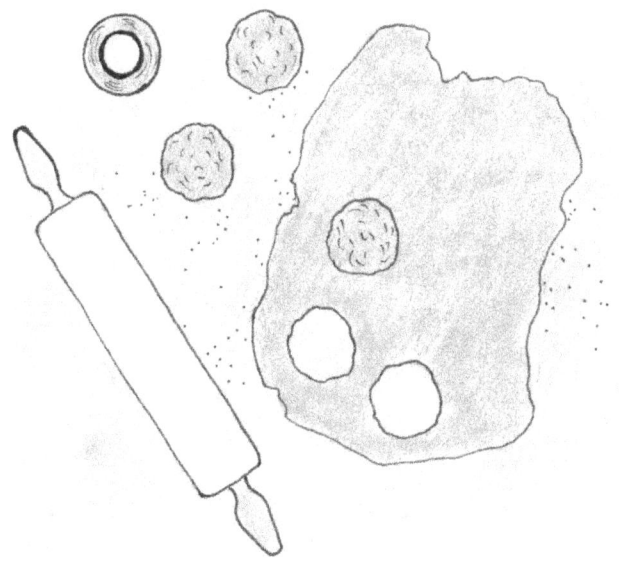

to the uncle who hit us

His first thought in the morning:
the needle. The small plastic bag.
How to heat it. How to
get it into his veins.
Even with his shame, it's easier
to think of this
than his mother, just buried.
His sister, slipping, her mind
a loose chain on a crooked cog.
She'll ask the same questions
again   again   again   again
and in the space between
he looks for purchase, a stone
strong enough to bear his weight.

I admire it. His devotion to my mother.
The bravery it takes just to wake up.

the rabbit also comes at dusk

None of this has been designed
with him in mind.

Not the feeder, strung high
nor the bird bath, heated

to a feather-friendly fifty degrees.
Not the way the fence stands,

vigilant and absolute, with no holes
for a quick escape. There are no

bushes or tall grass, within
which he can hide.

And yet he comes, happily, finding
the yard quiet, emptied.

He eats. He rolls his gray body
in the soft grass.

The birds have gone home
for the evening. The cats, too,

called for their nightly meals.
The dogs have gone,

seeking their warm beds.
It doesn't seem to matter,

(to the rabbit) that darkness .
is nearly here. Maybe I, too,

can find some peace
in this mismanaged world.

II.

wheel of fortune

    spiratio
A birth
    Impossible before

      aspiration

spiritus

The stuff of dreams (until)
    perspiration makes it flesh

(turning)

spiritus
spiratio
spirare
spiration

(turning)

    Idea. Birth. Blood.   (turning)

This will make you whole.

mary oliver

The poet is dead and I'll miss her.
I read her *best of* collections and suppose
this is more truthful

than any biography. Poetry tells all.
Who else was with her
in the quiet moments that create a life?

No one.
We live only when we are alone.

Poetry *only* was with her,
in a breath before the sun rose,
in the hand that stirred a coffee,

in the steam rising,
in the last light of that switch flicked *click*.

That is when Truth comes
knocking. In the early hours,
in a silent house, haunted by ghosts both

living and dead. So come close, dear friend.
Tell me everything. Tell me

what crossed
her mind as she closed her eyes to sleep.

Tell me what she dreamed of, longed for.
Tell me if she

finally found the answers to any of this.

does it matter

I write my words and throw them
into the wind. Should they hit
their mark, pull tears from an eye,
or clog the ventricles of some still-
beating heart—what of it?

Dust does not last. I will not
be here when the sun rises
one morning, purple.
Or one nightfall, black.

No mark, however deep, is immune
to time. And all
poems are written in dust, all longing
inscribed on paper

that must be fed to an open flame.
The most sturdy stone crumbles.
Entire heavens are destroyed
in gamma bursts before I sit down
to tea and a blackberry scone.

Why am I doing this?

Why must I bend down with cupped
hands in offering, pleading, begging
this dry earth for deliverance
that cannot last.

father

he lives in a little box. Confined.
Breathing is barely possible
let alone the turning of one's head
to see what might be *more*.

Does he never glimpse it?
The green over his shoulder,
that vast, vast beyond?

I wonder…
I can only wonder. Now
that I've left him behind. I had to.

The work of forgiving
can only be done under an open sky.

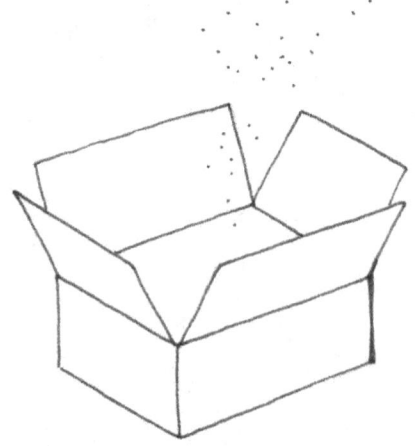

forgiveness

I withdraw the knife
and find the fruit rotted through.

Inside what is left, a worm
burrowing—a dissatisfaction.

If only I could stop biting into this,
the truth would be made clear:

He is only trying to live, too.

go on

I stand at the base of the mountain.
I stand there screaming into the snow.
My throat burns with bitterness

and hollow lack.
What is left of the past:
A shaking body, vibrating with need.

That's it.
Will doesn't exist.
It's a lie we tell children.

But every rebirth is a commitment,
a terrifying promise,
to give from nothing, *more*.

My vessel has reached the mountain,
but it can carry my spirit no further.
So the spirit calls out.

And is answered.
All that hungers comes.
From the mountain's shadow, emerges

a slinking lynx, a big-horned ram,
the coal-rimmed eyes of a cougar.
And I am an easy meal.

There is no hiding what I am.
Ignorance. Cowardice.
But consumed by a will all the same—

Or the fantasy of a will. A story. A fairytale
wielded against long winter nights.
I stand knee-deep in the snow.

I stand and come forward, hollow.
I want only to end. All of this.
But the jaws do not snap. The hooves

don't stamp me out. What is left of me
is not devoured.
And so now, I'm not alone.

3:16 a.m.

It's been scratching at the window
all night. The roof creaks. Large paws
shred shingles. Teeth gnaw
at the gutters. The bed
meant to cradle and support me
is as afraid as I am. It trembles. It sinks
with me in it. We go on like this for…
I don't know how long.

There is genius in desperation,
bravery too. And I,
unable to take anymore, throw back
the covers and open the window.
Come in already! Come in, damn you!

And it does.

A strange bird no larger than my heart.
It circles the room, screeching, taking
measure of this perimeter. And that's it.

It wants only to be inside.
It will be gone by first light.

what's going to happen

It's April at last. Winter is over
but this is no better.

Gunmetal gray
clouds and a listless sky

roll over the soaked earth.
The sun's flirtation is cold.

Hail pelts the slanted roof.
A crocus blooms.

A rabbit tears it apart.
A blue jay rubs his beak

on a bare magnolia branch,
seems to smell the pink blossoms

forming. A squirrel rolls
in the birdbath. Shivers.

And I have these bills,
one laid on top of the other.

The Visa is filling up,
while the good numbers keep going

down. In every season, choices
must be made. But *now*

the hail has ended and the sun
is warming up. The crocus

are still rising, joined
by the tenacious nubs

of white hyacinths. I suppose *now*
is a good a time as any for hope.

we do what we can

This morning I cleaned my house and thought
of soldiers, wounded. A festering
hidden in the dark. It happens, unavoidable.
But they want to fight, so they wrap their injuries
tight, add slow stealth to their gait and go on.
Lifting the damp cloth to the window, I realize
one can go on like this for a long time.
Until they drop. Until their comrades catch
the stench of infection, see the growing rot
snake black up the leg. If one is brave enough
to peel back the bandage, they'll say, "I
didn't know it was this bad—did you know
it was this bad?" Heads shake all around.
She'll lose the leg, of course.
If she doesn't do something now.
Remove the bandages. Open the clean window.
Write a poem.
Do something—anything—to let in the light.

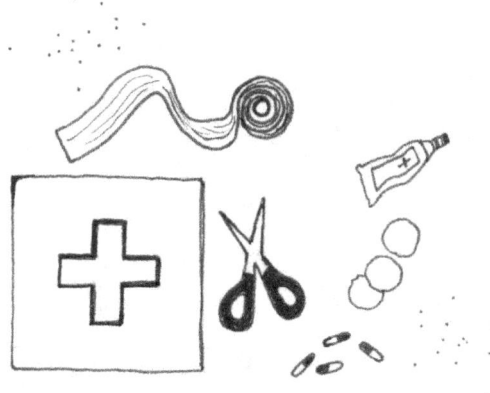

roulette

I fill the feeder, litter the ground.
I'm placing seeds that I believe
will draw the vibrant jays, swift
chickadees, sweet juncos, and soft
downies that I want.

I watch.
I wait.

First, a squirrel. Then a rabbit.
Chipmunks chasing tails.
A red-bellied woodpecker.
A flock of murderous finches.
A surprise flash of gold.

We don't decide or control
what visits us.   Or when.
This is as true in life as
it is in the body   and the mind.

divination

Turn over a tarot card. Chart the stars.
Let go of the possum bones clenched in your fist

and see where they fall. Count
the croaks of a toad on the pool's edge.

Number the geese passing overhead.
How many deer are lying down in the field?

Spilled salt. A crack in the pavement.
Does the milk-white moon wax or wane?

With our hands in the dirt,
counting clover, looking for certainty, a sign,

for answers of any kind. We're listening.
We're waiting for you to speak. Unfathomable,

the idea, we should do any of this
with our eyes closed tight.

settle in for the long haul

The woodpecker with his red crest
is at it again. What else can he do?

The magic of early morning,
of formless possibility is spent.

He's left with only the drudgery of
the day. He settles into his rhythm.

He continues as if he understands
just because you want something

it doesn't mean you're entitled to it.

And why not stay busy? Why not
carry on? I suspect that he knows

better than most what
unleashed hunger does to a heart.

hyacinth

The woman asked me for one
milk-white bloom.

And I, stunned into silence, fell
still. In the wind around me,
I turned the question over.

Over like my petals folded,
protecting eyes meant
to witness all. I was silent
long after she left me
untouched.

It doesn't matter the light
has changed now—

I've changed now. The right
question will do that to you.

And who could imagine
I had anything left to give?

first light

There is a doe. She steps
quietly over the low fence,
under the stretched blanket
of snow and night. She works
like this, unnoticed, unhurried
eating away
all that's overgrown,
taking all that can be taken.

Humble.
I only know that she's worked
me over, stripped me bare, once
morning comes. And bending
down, I can see her delicate
tracks in the fresh snow.

yet here I am, here I am reaching

My tongue is not shell shaped.
My lips rebuke such sharp curves,

yet here I am, here I am reaching

for my little music box, tuning
it to the notes of *illongo, francais,* 日本語.

I place a blue filter over the red one,
yellow upon blue—give me

the colors I know are there, but
can't yet see, let alone ~~describe~~ share.

yet here I am, here I am reaching

for the pen again. Turn the page over.
Look up at the sky as if

the answers will rain down
from above.

yet here I am, here I am reaching

for the story of his friend
who spoke six languages. Her world

must've been a pinwheel spinning.
A bright carnival.

She had not only all the colors,
but the smell of popcorn, the taste

of spun sugar against her lips, salty
grit under her nails.

At 87, when they took her to the home
she had only three languages left.

At 88, one. When the music stopped
and they closed the casket, none at all—

yet here I am, here I am reaching

for the world's flimsy blue handle,
never enough

because the force of living breaks us open,
it breaks us free,

and there can be nothing in these hands,
not where I am going.

—yet here I am, here I am reaching—

knowing is a mask (fear wears)

I've come all this way and found
nothing. Worse than nothing.
I walk

into the same room again. It's
as I left it. Or not. Did I leave
a scarf on the back of that chair?
Was it red for that matter?

Could it be that the room,
in my absence, has changed?
Or have I? It's very possible

I've never really looked before.
It's very possible,
I've wandered into the wrong
room. Let's assume the universe

really is large enough
to hold all these truths in its hands
at once. The truth flies

from the palm like a bird,
but for now it's here. For now
the room has changed and it hasn't.
The woman has changed and hasn't.
The distance changed her

and yet there was also no distance.

*The woman...her...*I'm doing it again.

All right. I can see this won't work
if there is anything left between us.

But you must meet me halfway.
And forgive me. It's so hard

to undress in front of you, when all
I have left clothing me are questions.

no carry-on baggage

What do you mean I can't bring this?
Don't you know how long it took me
to pack all of this up? In here,
I have every breakup text, every
love letter, every chapped-skin
embarrassment I could find. In here,
I have a CV twenty-years long.
I have every half-finished story and scrap
of shitty poetry. I have a whole
novel about horny werewolves, never shared.
I have unborn children, named. Every
apology (most of them mine) collected.
I have the nights my mother didn't
come home. My father's belt. Every
dirty needle and a stadium's worth of alcohol.
I have every time I've lifted a phone
and found there was no number worth calling.
Nowhere to spend Christmas.
No lock on the door.
I have failures, chipped, and cracked
with jagged seams. I have gallons,
and I do mean *gallons* of tears. Do you know
how long it takes to collect *gallons* of tears?
And I have lists. So many lists.
Of addresses where I've lived,
of celebrities I would sleep with if given
the chance, of books I want to read

and foods I've eaten, and a list of my
preferences, too. For green tea by a rainy
window. For the soft snore of a pug on my lap.
For exactly two feather pillows, and
desserts made of thick sweet cream. Or melted
chocolate. For Parisian cafes, and wandering old cities
Museums that look like clocks. For the smell
of coffee, but the taste of tea.
Robins singing in the twilight. The sound
of someone I love coming home.
For the fragrant, flowering trees of spring.
For snow falling thick. For stars shining and a moon
hung just right. For thick socks. For piles of books,
for my hands tripping across a piano,
for boys who are prettier than girls.
And all the girls, too, of course. One in particular.
The kisses…

Not even those? Not even *one* kiss?
A *very* good kiss?

Oh, no, I didn't read the fine print.

Permitted: only what's light enough to carry.
Ah, I see. Well, then.

I'm going to need your help
taking out all of the rest.

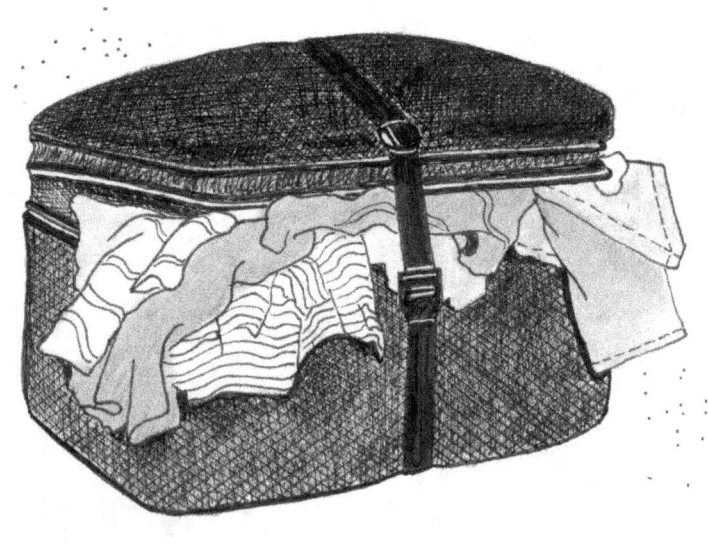

III.

you called to ask for money again

There is a Buddhist parable
about a loving mother, armless,
whose child falls into the river.

She has no choice.
She rushes alongside the thrashing
water. Her legs carry her

as fast as they can over the unforgiving
rocks and earth. As the sky watches,
as the grass sleeps. As the world,

indifferent or unaware, carries on.
It matters only that she stays. That she
doesn't leave or walk away. But oh…

how it must have hurt. This hatchet
to the chest, to the lungs, to all the air
leaving in the torrent of

a winter's breeze. How her heart,
wing-pinned, must have floundered,
breathless. A fish flopping

up against the rough shore.
But I am the mother here.
You the child. We changed places

decades ago. A tragedy, really, that
even now, having been so hollowed out
by your hunger, by your hatchet fists,

I'm still ready to throw all of me,
every last piece, into the rushing stream.
I suppose it only matters that I don't.

when pride lifts her mask

It's Unworthiness I see.
Imagine my surprise.
Fiery hair and flamboyant
cheekbones that cut.
An imperial glare
that makes the bravest
step back. The strong jaw
and tall, straight spine.
Her claws, half-cocked—
all of it stripped down

to the mere sprig of a girl.
Small arms clutch her
stomach. Her eyes hold
more fear than color. I
can tell she's been neglected
for a long time.
But her dirty, cracked nails
tell me she's a fighter.
And that's enough for me.

I invite her inside. I offer
her a seat at the table, a cup
of tea. I want to know her better.
I want her to break and mend
my heart. But she runs.
Or maybe I'm the one running.

imperfect

There comes a terrible moment,
when one realizes that all the grief
around them, is their own doing.

Maybe this was not always so.

Maybe it was a song started by another
and you, the dutiful, sung your notes
long after the others had stopped.

But that still leaves you with the *after*,
a long, summer afternoon that seems
more dream than awake. The sand
in the hourglass suspended, waiting
for you to begin again. But you can't.

Cleaning out the room reveals
the years of neglect, just how much
you've tucked away, overlooked,
forgotten. It gives the impression
that your work will never be done.

If you sort this, someone else—maybe you—
will come in and mess it up again.

They'll leave their shoes in front of the door.
They'll leave a sweating water glass

directly on the tabletop. The dust
will settle. It's enough to drive anyone mad.

And what if that's the point?

Not to be finished—never to arrive.
Simply to have your little room in the world
and to love it. To care for it, to live
in its imperfect swell and flux,
to open the windows on warm days, cold
days, rainy days. To let in what would come in.
To clear out what must go out.

All of it, either way, done with a gentle,
patient hand. And the first notes of song—
a new tune, certainly—
whistled through your glad heart.

the wisdom of no escape

I suspect old age is a gift.
Perhaps terrible illness, too.

Why else would we surrender
our bodies, our lives, or

all this desire
unless we were drowning

in pain? Even then, I know
it would take a long time.

Little to nothing else could
make me ready to relinquish

myself to the unknowable.
Not that I haven't tried:

religion. Atheism. Mantras.
Hot yoga on Sundays.

Tarot cards. Moon charts.
An abundance of

chocolate cake. It's inevitable
we should want to see

the fine print before
signing it all away.

No one has come back
after all. Or they did

bearing tales of white light
and old, friendly faces.

But who can believe them?
There are too many

variables. I want to know
how far did you really go?

Any waiting room might
seem nice with the right

people in it. This says
nothing of the man

with the knives and needles
behind the door. Or maybe it's

the retelling itself. *I saw it.
It's beautiful. It's*

everything we've hoped for.
We don't have to be afraid.

Desperation rings
through the air like a bell.

this

This will never come again.
This woman sitting at this desk. This typewriter
    fingering this melody, this bird song in flight
careening out the open window.

            Bittersweet love
of what I have, of what will be lost. A longing
            certainly. But the rest is smoke and vapors.
The rest—
                dreams torn in two, irreparable
                    upon waking.

god

I am working in the garden.
I'm always working. You can't

have as many irons in the fire,
or galaxies in a palm, as I do, and know

of something called *rest*. You invented
the sabbath, not me.

Flowers always need pruning. Wayward
vines must be cut back. The dirt

wants to be lifted from the weight
of itself. And my children

sometimes wander. As I work,
a frog leaps into the rose's thorns.

A spider crawls across my hand.
I set each on a better path—

I believe. But how often
they mistrust my directions.

mala

Picasso jasper
minute planetary moons
each strung & expanding.

To deepen meditation,
hold a moon between your fingers.
Count a breath.

In.
Out.

And name the passing starships
of your mind

Thinking.

God has done this.
Rolling each creation between
deft fingers, wondering

what might come of it,
once this work is done.

you can't keep it

The tight shape of your body, or it misplaced youth.
There aren't enough pushups in this world for what's
coming.
Your teeth, however well brushed,
have a best buy date. The spine will compress. The fingers
will twist in on themselves. Your bones will creak like un-
oiled
hinges. Likewise, the nice car you bought will rust, rattle.
The tires,
too, will wear down. *POP*. The little dog on your lap now
has gray in his muzzle. Your ears will hear fewer
and fewer notes. Tea will turn to gallstones,
your once lush hair will thin. The world is
becoming a soft Monet painting,
set up at a distance. The cooing
of doves, all that beautiful bird song, lost.
The blue jay screeching past the window,
no matter how vibrant, will live only seven
or ten years more. How many more
mornings with your wife, with coffee
and kisses placed by the ear.
Forget the money. Forget
the good opinion of others.
Forget your best memories.
Time makes dreams of
everything: of this house,
of the sunflowers rising,

of the violet light turning blue,
of skin splitting open
to let the pressure out.
A winter is forming
snow-white on the horizon.
To receive any gift,
especially a gift
of this magnitude,
a clenched
hand must
first
open
up.

reincarnation

As with any long journey
that takes you far from home
it's essential to pack light.

You can only carry so much.

First, shed one's memories.
Then self-evident truths and all
hard-earned knowledge.
One hundred percent off, no returns.

Believe in nothing, but the power of
unzipping your skin, your mind. Don't try
to catch what's spilling out, rushing
away from *you*.

Easier said than done.
It doesn't help to know that

once upon a time, we were one
spirit, a single mass in the cosmos. But
nothing lasts forever. A collision, a catalyst
and every part of ourselves thrown
outward, spiraling through space.

What was as close to me as my own
pounding heart, pounding fists, tender

blinking eyelids, rushed away from me.
The distance ever expanding. Still.

Of course this separation breeds conflict.
Of course the trauma makes strangers
of us all. And in my isolation, I hear only
my own voice, saying the same empty
words, echoing. Call this eternity.

And as any fool, I hold the erroneous belief
I'm all that's left of me. And you there,
on the other side of the line, are unrecognizable.

the merits

Sure, first you must give it all up.
Shed your skin, your pain, go
white-eyed like a milk snake
and crack yourself open. Slither
into something new. But then...

To bite into a warm August peach
for the first time. To feel the feather
light brush of lips for the first time.

To fall backward, arms open
into the pond behind your parents' house—
better parents—and when you crash
that bike, wailing on the pavement,
you'll look up and see the hand offered.
The surprise, the jolt, because it's never
the hand you expected. Your first friend.
And the dear friends you recognize
every time, in every life.

To be rid of these bones, after they've ached
for forty years—look at you now!

Running full speed down the dirt lane,
a dog you love more than your own
two hands yipping beside you.
Laughter in your ears. The apple-blossom

wind blows back your hair.

To have it all *new* again, and again.
To redo or undo as you please.
Even with the checks to write
and accounts to balance—

we still get it all. With enough courage,
it can be done. With enough heart,
you will hear it, warm in the glow of

a porchlight,
the voice that keeps calling you home.

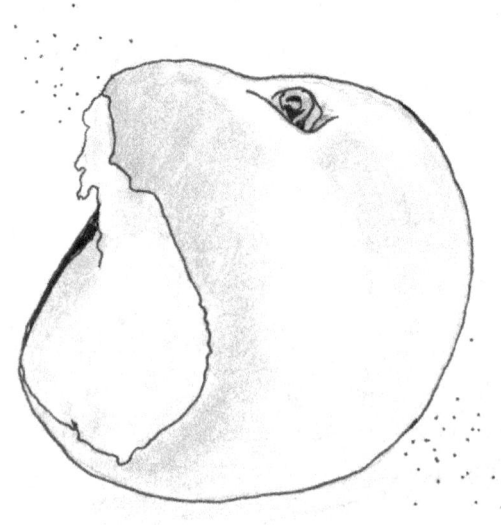

snow in april

Hot—for a week.
I was wearing *flip flops* in the neighborhood.
My little dog, ears up, trotting alongside me
to the rhythm of *this is more like it*.

Winters in Michigan are long, true,
like dreams that begin in your mother's kitchen,
1980s, all big hair, cigarette smoke and
fried bologna in a pan. It goes on like that

until bill after bill is flying through the mail slot.
The envelopes are knee high now, waist-high
as you swim in search of a checkbook,
the beating heart of a pen.

When the world turns on you like this,
when it folds itself into unrecognizable shapes,
shows you the sharp points of its hidden teeth,
don't hold on. Don't obsess

about the smiles you thought you were having.
Instead, pull the chair to the window.
Bring the warm mug, too. Settle into this.
And watch it all come down.

surrender

Why is this so difficult?
Why must the sweaty, half-mad

fever of fear rise in me,
and always when my hands dare

to relax their hold on all the little
treasures, trinkets I've gathered up.

Why can't I give up,
give myself over, the way a leaf turns

over? Why can't I do it splendidly,
a deep rich green sliding

into gold? The way little children
will spin and spin and spin

their arms open, twirling,
their laughter escaping them

at the seams. Damn the balance.
There's only wild delight

in abandonment. They've only room
for wide-eyed excitement, waiting,

hungry for what magic the world
will pull from her sleeve next.

I want to live like that.
I want to love like that.

When swollen clouds break open
with electricity, when the ocean

tilts suddenly to the left,
when the ship's whistle sounds,

don't let me count what has been lost,
only what's been returned. Let each bit

of hard-earned gold, though cherished, be
tossed into the waters below.

With a smile, bold, spreading
like a new horizon across my lips.

ode to winter

Step into the cold night, into the wind,
which isn't the wind, but
a metaphor for the moving world.

It bites.
It nips at all exposed flesh, usually
your hands. Its aim is to render you
motionless, unable to lift a pen—
or dig your way to salvation.

You don't know how long it's been waiting.
The moonlit hills were designed
as mirrors to show you who
you really are, what followed you

into this place. Don't be afraid
of ghosts or demons. Both
are of your own making. Instead, fall back
into the snow. Give yourself completely

to the starry sky above. Perhaps it's a comfort
to know we all end here.

You're not alone. Or if you are,
you won't be for long. There are others
on the path now. Their voices are soft,

their breath fog white.

But you don't have to get up and greet them.
You don't have to do anything, any longer.
Lay there, baby, and enjoy the wonder.

This is your moment.
The universe put this one together for you.

All of it:
the shooting star,
the distant rumble,
even that unbearable ache in your chest.

This nocturnal serenade was a million
years in the making. And now
the moon, the stars, and all their attendants
stand against the wall, waiting, longing.

They pray that maybe,
finally, at long last, you'll join the dance.

author's note

Dear reader,

I hope you enjoyed this collection. If you would be so kind, please leave a review for it on whichever retail sites you prefer.

It would mean so much to me, and to the other poetry lovers who may discover this collection because of your review. Not to mention reviews are one of the best ways to support the writers and artists you love.

If you want more poems, you can visit me at
https://www.korymshrum.com/free-starter-library

For more art from the amazing, Victoria Solomon, you can follow her on Instagram @victoriamsolomon

On my website, you can also sign up for my newsletter and receive a free poetry chapbook. The newsletter will be sent 2-3 times a month and contain free poems and updates about my work. I will never share your email and, of course, you can unsubscribe at any time.

Hope to chat with you soon!

k.b. marie

also by k.b. marie

birds & other dreamers

questions for the dead

you can't keep it

about the author

K.B. Marie has published over thirty poems in magazines such as *Bateau, North American Review, Ascent,* and elsewhere under the name, Kory M. Shrum. She earned her MFA at Western Michigan University and has worked for *New Issues Press, Zone 3 Press,* and *Third Coast Literary Magazine.*

For ten years, she taught writing to thousands of university students before deciding to write full-time. Her favorite kind of poetry combines art and words – which is why her work is often accompanied with illustrations or other visuals.

She lives in Michigan with her equally well-read wife, Kimberly, and their rescue pug, Charley.

Anything else you'd like to know can be found at https://www.korymshrum.com/poetry

about the illustrator

Victoria Solomon is a Michigan-based artist specializing in pencil and ink portraiture and other art. When not powering through nursing school, she loves to experiment with new art supplies and write fiction. She also makes an incredible chocolate cake. Victoria shares her home with her husband and her small brood of children and cats.

Follow her on Instagram @victoriamsolomon

www.ingramcontent.com/pod-product-compliance
Lightning Source LLC
Chambersburg PA
CBHW052109110526
44592CB00013B/1537